BARRON'S

1000

CAT NAMES

It's the name that really makes a kitten into an unmistakable individual. It's even better if this name is based on the kitten's appearance or personality. In this guide you will find the best and most popular names for cats, and much more. Of course you'll learn the origins of those names as well.

Contents

WHAT NAMING A CAT IS ALL ABOUT

The Wider the Choice, the Harder It Is   5

The Secret of the Right Name   6

Info: Nicknames Are in Demand   6

Tip: Changing the Name   7

Test: What Is My Cat's Personality Type?   8

Real VIPs—Famous Cats   10

Celebrities and Their Feline Friends   11

HOW CATS LEARN TO UNDERSTAND US   12

Pedigreed Cats—of Noble Lineage?   14

Special Feature: Cat Horoscope   15

TEACHING A CAT ITS NAME   16

THE BEST
CAT NAMES FROM A TO Z

THE BEST NAMES FOR MALES   **20**

Ten Very Common Cat Names for Males
and Females   20

Cute Names for Black Tomcats   22

Imaginative Names for Twosomes   24

Good Names for Princes and Princesses   27

THE BEST NAMES FOR FEMALES   **33**

Fine-Sounding Names for White Beauties   33

Good Names for Sensitive Creatures   36

Good Names for Sociable Felines   40

Suitable Names for Long-haired Cats   43

Nice Names for Red Pussycats   44

APPENDIX

Index   46

Addresses   47

WORTH KNOWING AND FUNNY

You will find stories about cats on pages 21, 23, 25, 26, 28, 29, 30, 31, 32, 34, 35, 37, 38, 39, 41, 42, and 45.

What Naming a
Cat
Is All About

Often cats' names tell us more about their owners than about the cats themselves. For example, someone who is fond of Mozart is apt to choose Amadeus, and since the film *Pretty Woman* appeared, a lot of cats have been named Julia. Everything is permissible. Even a favorite food may be reflected in your pet's name.

The Wider the Choice, The Harder It Is

The possibilities are really limitless when it comes to choosing a name that really fits your beloved furry monster.

Some people base their choice on great historical names such as Napoleon, Caesar, or Cleopatra—imposing figures that stand for strength, power, and beauty. Others name their cats for famous actors, such as Julia (Roberts) or Leonardo (Di Caprio), or for athletes such as Tiger (Woods) or the soccer star Mia (Hamm).

The names of comic-strip heroes such as Tom (and Jerry) or Garfield are also popular. Especially trendy now are names from other cultures. To our ears, they sound exotic and mysterious. One such example: "Aponi" comes from a Native American language and is translated as "Butterfly." But what does your cat think about its name? Probably it couldn't care less. Only one thing is certain: Cats learn one- and two-syllable names most quickly, and they react especially well to names that you can pronounce in tender, come-hither tones (see page 16). But it can definitely be more unusual than Kitty or Pussycat.

The Secret of the Right Name

Names change the world. Names lend personality, make getting along and communicating easier, and allow strangers to become friends. Names are vehicles for feelings and desires; they strengthen our bonds with other people and with animals.

When it comes to our house pets, the name is a symbol of the trust and affection between human and animal. We unconsciously assign a different value to an animal that has a name: It is transformed from a "thing" into a fellow creature and a partner. Once you have chosen a cat to share your home, you share your life with it. It is a friend, confidant, and source of comfort for families, children, single adults, and senior citizens. The cat's name should express all of that: closeness and affection, belonging and dependability. But it needs to express much more as well: the name should be well suited to its bearer, of course, should do justice to the cat's appearance and personality, and—as far as possible—should also take into account its individual characteristics.

The name will stick: Have you taken everything into consideration?

Names should be custom-tailored. This is what you need to keep in mind when selecting a name:

➤ Your cat will learn a one- or two-syllable name especially quickly (see Teaching a Cat Its Name, page 16).

➤ It's not what you say, but how you say it: The inflection is what matters when you're praising or scolding. Long, drawn-out vowels guarantee your kitty's attention.

➤ The name should be accepted by the entire family and by everyone else who spends time with the cat.

➤ Avoid names that are really embarrassing.

INFO
NICKNAMES ARE IN DEMAND

The cat has become a full member of the family. Nicknames are the symbol of the more intense relationship and an expression of our affection.

➤ As nicknames we like to use the terms "Sweetie," "Honey," "Baby," and the like.

➤ Keep in mind that your little tiger also has to learn its nickname, if it is markedly different from its given name.

➤ For these reasons, decide on only one nickname, if at all possible. Too many names will just confuse the cat.

> This is the very model of an adventurous male. Nothing is safe from this cat. His name ought to express that as well. How about calling him Crazy or Nutty?

TIP

CHANGING THE NAME

Even if a cat—for example, an older cat from the pet shelter—already has a name, you can "rechristen" your puss if you don't like the name. To do so, follow the procedures described on page 16 ff.

It may be intended as witty, but who wants to call Piggy or Little Pooper to come in from the yard or from elsewhere in the apartment so that everyone can hear?

➤ Don't forget: People who are celebrities today may already be "out" tomorrow, but your cat will have the name for the rest of its life.

➤ Small children frequently can't pronounce complicated or long names correctly. Thus simple, clear names such as Betty, Suzy, Tom, or Billy are called for in this case.

➤ Decide on one name. If there is a short form or a nickname, then pick one of the two. Many different names, including nicknames, will just confuse your cat.

➤ A cat's name should not call up any negative associations. Otherwise, you will transfer unpleasant memories of people or situations to the cat.

➤ Please don't pick any names that are taboo. Cats' names, like any other names, should not insult anyone; therefore, it's probably best to avoid naming your cat after controversial figures, like politicians.

➤ True, your cat won't understand the meaning of its name, but its name should not be demeaning to it.

Prince and Princess

They expect unconditional homage. And it's taken for granted that everyone can read their every wish in their eyes.

Smarty and Softy

"Sweet" and "very cuddly" are the words you could use to describe this type. Such cats don't think much of heroics, however.

Sensitive Little Creatures

Sensitive, easily offended, and a little fearful. The "tender little souls" of the cat world, they are suitable only for considerate people.

What Is My Cat's

➤ The only acceptable place to rest is the bed.
➤ The cat protests if you are inattentive.
➤ It can't stand anything other than its usual food.
➤ It occupies your favorite armchair.
➤ It demands that you adapt yourself to it.

➤ It immediately notices if you're not feeling well.
➤ It loves to cuddle.
➤ It is cautious about new things, but not negative.
➤ It follows your every step.
➤ It almost never uses its claws.

➤ It makes itself scarce when the children are making a lot of noise.
➤ It doesn't want to share your attention.
➤ It hates hectic activities.
➤ Its feelings are hurt when you yell at it.
➤ It loves its familiar surroundings.

List of names on page 27

List of names on page 29

List of names on page 36

Lovable Adventurer

They are receptive to new things. They have no objection to variety in their daily routines. Better too much than too little.

The Eternal Child

Indoor cats in particular remain eternal children where we are concerned. They are playful, very affectionate, and enjoy our attention.

The Sociable Feline

The term "peace-maker" is also used. These cats do not like to live alone, and they try to ensure harmony in a group of cats.

Personality Type?

➤ New toys are immediately investigated.
➤ This cat enjoys playing boisterous games with you.
➤ It suffers if it's not allowed to go outdoors.
➤ It sniffs at you with interest, even if you've just been petting a dog.
➤ It loves having visitors.

List of names on page 32

➤ It's always in the mood for a little game with you.
➤ It insists that meals be served on time.
➤ It enjoys a soothing massage.
➤ It likes to lick your hands and arms.
➤ It's always giving you "nose kisses."

List of names on page 34

➤ It gets along well with other cats.
➤ It has a "bad conscience" when you fuss at it.
➤ It settles disputes in a group of cats.
➤ It understands if you don't have time for it just now.
➤ It hates discord.

List of names on page 40

Real VIPs – Famous Cats

Cats are obstinate and independent, have a casual elegance, and are complete individualists by nature. It's not surprising, then, that they have long been a source of inspiration for writers and caricaturists.

Sir Walter Scott, author of *Ivanhoe,* claimed that "Cats are a mysterious kind of folk. There is more passing in their minds than we are aware of." And Mark Twain once said that "If a man could be crossed with a cat, it would improve the man but deteriorate the cat."

Charles Baudelaire, Heinrich Heine, Rainer Maria Rilke, and Oscar Wilde, too, were intensely interested in cats and wrote poems about them. Edgar Allan Poe used his cat, Catarina, as the basis for one of his stories, "The Black Cat." A house cat, Catarina provided warmth and comfort to Poe's dying wife when the author could not afford to have her tuberculosis treated by a doctor.

Then there's the comic-strip cat Sylvester, the greedy tom whose intended snack, the little bird Tweety Pie, repeatedly eludes him. Sylvester is the creation of the Hollywood studios of Warner Brothers. Think of Tom and Jerry, who are permanently at war with each other. The two managed to win seven Oscars in Hollywood. And who didn't cry when the butler tried to cheat Disney's Aristocat Duchess and her sweet little kittens of their

TIP
NAMES FOR SEVERAL CATS

If you have several cats, you need to choose names that can't be confused with each other. Naming three cats Huey, Dewey, and Louie like the three little ducks in Disney's Donald Duck shorts may sound cute to our ears, but to cats these names are indistinguishable. The cats won't be able to tell them apart, and all three are likely to come racing up at once when you call one of the names. That can be irritating in the long run. It's better to pick clearly distinguishable names that are a good match for your pets' personalities and temperaments.

inheritance? Then, of course, there's Garfield, the rude, lazy cat created by Jim Davis.

For more than 20 years, audiences have been enthusiastic about the musical *Cats.* Composer Andrew Lloyd Webber's lyrics were based on the cat poems of T. S. Eliot, a Nobel Prize laureate in literature. There are many examples demonstrating that cats offer wonderful material for books, films, or cartoons, even for the zeitgeist. Just think of comic-strip figures such as Fritz the Cat, the tomcat whose main interests are good times and sex. In the prudish America of the 1960s, he symbolized free love.

Celebrities and Their **Feline Friends**

Mark Twain, author of *Tom Sawyer* and *Huckleberry Finn,* was a great admirer of cats who purposely picked bizarre names for his pets. The names Blatherskite, Beelzebub, Appollinaris, Sour Mash, and Zoroaster were among those that he chose for his cats, allegedly to give little children practice with hard-to-pronounce names.

Ernest Hemingway, the eccentric writer and Nobel Prize laureate, kept about 30 cats at his Finca Vigía in Cuba. He was fascinated by the animals. A quote from one of his works says that "Cats easily succeed in doing what we humans fail to achieve: going through life without making any noise." Even today, cats continue to roam his estate. Doris Lessing, one of England's most famous women writers, lives with her cat Yum-Yum in London. She also wrote a book about living with cats: *Particularly Cats.*

Many famous people have proclaimed their love of cats, saying they could not imagine life without their furry friends. Among them are actors such as Victoria Principal, Valerie Bertinelli, Claudia Cardinale, and Sophia Loren; famous painters such as Pablo Picasso; the scientist Albert Einstein; statesmen such as Bill Clinton and Winston Churchill; philosophers such as Sir Isaac Newton; and, of course, writers such as Patricia Highsmith, a masterful writer of mysteries who loved her cats more than people. The list of cat-loving writers in particular could be continued ad infinitum.

Charles Dickens had a cat named Willamena who had a litter of kittens. Although Dickens had originally decided to give away the kittens to other people, he grew very fond of one of the females. He kept this cat, calling her Master's Cat. She sat at his side as he wrote his books, putting out his candle when she wanted his attention. Harriet Beecher Stowe, author of *Uncle Tom's Cabin,* took in a stray cat that she named Calvin, who often sat on her shoulder while she worked. Stowe wrote some of her most famous prose with him perched there.

How Cats Learn to Understand Us

CATS AND HUMANS: MAKING IT WORK

A cat and a human are an odd couple—and yet they get along extremely well. If the two are interested in each other and fond of each other, a way to communicate will quickly be found. To help make it a success, the cat, too, employs all its powers of observation and its special abilities.

On Familiar Terms with a Human

How is it possible that cats understand us so well? It's quite simple: The little creatures learn quickly and are close observers. The kitty learns its name (see page 16) in no time, but quite soon it acquires other words and even sentences as well, which it hears again and again in certain situations and in a certain tone of voice. Commands, too—such as "Come" or "No" (best delivered with a raised index finger)—can quickly be interpreted correctly by cats. Usually, only the obedience part is difficult, as cats are well known to be obstinate creatures.

To understand us, it is equally important for cats to pay attention to our body language, our gestures, and our facial expressions. Cats watch us so closely that sometimes you might think they have clairvoyant abilities. For example, you may still be sitting comfortably in your armchair but just thinking about standing up, when Kitty, with tail raised high, anticipates your intention and moves first. Can cats read humans' minds?

Little Amadeus is only four weeks old, but he already knows his humans. At the moment, however, Mama is still his favorite, because she's his milk source and it's so cozy and warm to snuggle next to Mama.

Almost seven weeks old, Alex and his brother Jingles are still in the imprinting phase. If the kittens have good experiences with humans now, they'll be especially affectionate later on.

Dawn is three months old. She gets along very well with her humans. The little gourmet knows exactly where the container of treats is kept, and by now she's also skillful enough to open it.

TIP
MISUNDERSTANDING

First Kitty insisted on being petted, but then it abruptly bit us painfully. Are cats treacherous? No, Kitty gave us a warning: "Enough!" The tip of its tail quivered, its pupils became enlarged, and it put its ears back. We just overlooked the unambiguous signals.

No, of course not. But your slightly tensed back muscles have revealed that you're about to get out of the chair. Maybe now Kitty will get that treat at last.

It is also surprising how responsive cats are to our moods. If we are depressed or ill, we couldn't wish for a more affectionate comforter. Often the pussycat will lie for hours next to us in bed,

even sacrifice its round of the house, or snuggle close to us, purring gently. In these situations, too, we probably are unconsciously sending out clear signals for the cat. It understands at once what state we are in at the moment and bestows on us the attention we need. Often, this concern for our well-being is enough to make us feel better.

13

Pedigreed Cats—
of Noble Lineage?

In the pedigrees of purebred cats, we often read such fine-sounding names as Anastasia von Bullerbue, Cleopatra from the Temple of Isis, and Agamemnon of the Wild Meadowland. Are these cats descended from ancient families of noble lineage?

No, of course not. It is true, however, that most purebred cats are from excellent stock, because responsible breeders mate only animals that have good genes and that possess the breed traits specified by breeders' associations. But the impressive cattery name tells us only which breeder the cat comes from.

Of course, every breeder wants to emphasize the breed characteristics of his or her cats by choosing an appropriate name, and, of course, the cats' origins should be clearly discernible, as far as possible.

Applying for a Cattery Name

Every cat breeder who belongs to a recognized breed association for purebred cats is entitled to apply for a cattery name issued by the association. In pedigrees, breeding certificates, show catalogs, and other official documents, the name of the cat always must be given in conjunction with the cattery name.

In the choice of a cattery name, almost no limits are placed on your imagination. Only a few rules have to be followed:

➤ The proposed cattery name must be submitted to a recognized breed association for purebred cats. You are allowed to suggest no more than two or three names.

➤ The cattery name may contain no more than 15 letters.

➤ The proposed cattery name can be rejected by the association if an identical or similar-sounding name is already registered, because confusion could result.

What the Stars Tell Us

CAT HOROSCOPE

ASTROLOGY:

Check and see whether Kitty's strengths and weaknesses are in keeping with its sign of the zodiac. You will find suitable names on pages 25, 31, 39, and 41.

➤ **Aries Cat**
March 21–April 19. Self-confident, high-spirited, open-minded, and quick to learn. Weaknesses: impatient and demanding; males are pugnacious.

➤ **Taurus Cat**
April 21–May 20. Devoted to the idle life, loves good food and its humans. Weaknesses: sometimes jealous and a little sluggish.

➤ **Gemini Cat**
May 21–June 21. Cheerful, adaptable, smart, and full of energy. Weaknesses: Its liveliness can be exasperating.

➤ **Cancer Cat**
June 22–July 22. Sensitive and playful. Loves to be on your lap. Weaknesses: easily offended and wildly jealous.

➤ **Leo Cat**
July 23–August 22. Likes to be the center of attention, trusting, friendly, becomes independent early. Weaknesses: stubborn unless it can rule the roost.

➤ **Virgo Cat**
August 24–September 22. Faithful, loving, likes things clear-cut and stable at home. Weaknesses: likes to keep a little distance, though the first impression is deceptive.

➤ **Libra Cat**
September 23–October 23. Loves harmony, tolerant, good-natured, likes a snug home. Weaknesses: sometimes indecisive in its behavior.

➤ **Scorpio Cat**
October 24–November 21. Very magnetic, affable, compassionate. Weaknesses: obstinate and passionately jealous.

➤ **Sagittarius Cat**
November 22–December 21. Sociable, friendly, easily satisfied, inventive, freedom-loving. Weaknesses: If it lacks challenge, it gets depressed.

➤ **Capricorn Cat**
December 22–January 19. Dependable, intelligent, fastidious. Weaknesses: vain and recalcitrant if things don't go its way.

➤ **Aquarius Cat**
January 20–February 18. Inventive, curious, and affectionate. Weaknesses: moody and quite willful. Doesn't like strangers.

➤ **Pisces Cat**
February 19–March 20. Sensitive, affectionate, intuitive. Weaknesses: jealous and definitely wants its own way, but not vindictive.

Teaching a Cat Its Name

HOW A CAT LEARNS TO ANSWER TO ITS NAME

Cats are intelligent and learn quickly. They are especially ready to learn if there is some benefit to be derived. We humans can take advantage of this situation. And that is why it's not at all difficult to teach Kitty to respond to its name in a jiffy.

Important: It's the Right Tone That Counts

It is true that cats answer quickly to two-syllable names. However, the theory that the name should contain a lot of "i" or "e" sounds is debatable. It is the tone in which you speak its name that matters most.

"Good bait catches fine fish." In a figurative sense, that is also true for your cat. Reward your pussycat at first with a little treat whenever you call it by name and it actually does come running.

It doesn't always have to be a treat. Most cats also appreciate being petted and hearing a fond tone in your voice. Always link calling your cat's name with petting it.

Learning Its Name

✔ Cats learn one- and two-syllable names such as Kim or Mimi especially quickly.

✔ Make sure the cat's name can't be confused with other words, as, for example, when you say "Come" to your cat named Tom.

✔ Don't constantly vary the nicknames you use. That will just confuse your cat.

✔ All the family members should agree on the cat's name and always use the same name when speaking to it.

✔ At first, be sure you never connect anything unpleasant for the cat with the sound of its name, such as being locked up or being given a dose of medicine.

If you succeed in calling your black male Othello or your imposing female Huntress in a coaxing, tender voice, then the cats will also cheerfully come running when they hear these names.

At first, you should always link calling the name with something positive for the cat. You can feed your kitty, give it plenty of petting, or offer it a much-coveted treat. Under no circumstances should your cat link the sound of its name with something unpleasant. However, you certainly can use a sharp tone on occasion to reprimand a transgressor. Kitty will not hold that against you, because it is well aware that it has done something wrong. By using the right tone, you can scold, entice, show affection, or even calm the cat.

The Best
Cat Names
from A to Z

Are you looking for an appropriate name for your male cat, female cat, or pair of cats? Then you're in the right place. In the following section of this guide, you will find 1000 traditional, exotic, famous, clever, common, and noble names. The right one for your favorite feline is sure to be among them.

Allow Me to Introduce Myself . . .

It's really not so easy to find the right name for your little pussycat. Most important, it has to suit the cat and sound good, and it has to be something the cat can learn as quickly as possible (see page 16). The following 1000 names from A to Z are a colorful mixture of melodious, unusual, famous, beautiful, and common names. You will see that the list of names contains many names from English and from Romance languages. There's a good reason for that,

because these names are usually short and sound especially fascinating. In the bonus lists you will find very common cat names, good names for twosomes, black tomcats, white beauties, red-haired and long-haired cats, and for individual zodiac signs and personality types such as Prince and Princess, Smarty and Softy, or the Eternal Child. The meanings of many of the names listed there are given in the general list of names for both male and female cats. Amusing stories about cats and the way they got their names demonstrate that cats are highly individual creatures with diverse temperaments and personalities.

The Best Names for **Males**

Ace *For a top-notch, first-rate cat*

Achilles *The hero in the Trojan war in Homer's* The Iliad

Acrobat *Greek for "walking on tiptoe"*

Adam *Means "from the earth," ideal for a firstborn kitten*

Ad lib *For the cat that acts extemporaneously, to improvise*

Admiral *High ranking, deserving of respect, admirable*

Adonis *A beautiful individual, the god of beauty, youth*

Aesop *Author of fables, a wise character*

Afro *For the cat with curly, fuzzy hair*

Al *Noble, illustrious, short for Albert*

Aladdin *From the story "Aladdin and the Magic Lamp"*

Alex *Defender of mankind, Alexander the Great*

Alf *A fun name meaning "Alien Life Form"*

Alibi *Good for a cat that's often in trouble and needs an excuse*

Alpha *Number one cat, dominant*

Ten Very Common Cat Names for Males and Females

Do you prefer names that are not likely to go out of fashion? Then you can choose among these. Here are 10 frequently used names for male and female cats:
Males: Bandit, Blackie, Charlie, Felix, Fritz, Jingles, Morris, Rebel, Scout, Tom.
Females: Goldie, Isis, Kitty, Lisa, Mimi, Missy, Pussy, Sheba, Suzy, Tabby.

Amadeus *Wolfgang Amadeus Mozart, composer of classical music*

Amaretto *Italian almond-flavored liqueur*

Ambros *Good name for a large, dark cat*

Amigo *Spanish for "friend"*

Amor *Roman god of love*

Andy *Short for Andrew, also André in French*

Angus *Outstanding, excellent, also Gus*

Antares *Large star in the Scorpio constellation*

Anthony *Variations Anton, Tony, Antonio*

Apache *Native American tribe, ideal for a cat with patches*

Apollo *Greek god of prophecy*

Archie *Noble and bold*

Ares *Greek god of war*

Argent *French for "silver"*

Argo *Greek for "fast, quick," the ship Jason sailed to find the Golden Fleece*

Argyle *Tartan or pattern from a clan tartan, also Argyll*

Aries *First sign of the zodiac, for a cat with a strong personality*

Aristotle *Famous Greek philosopher*
Arlo *Singer Arlo Guthrie*
Armani *Designer, fashion label*
Arthur *Celtic name, also Art, Arty*
Ash *Ideal name for a gray or grayish white cat, also Ashley*
Aspen *Good name for a golden-colored cat*
Astro *Meaning "star," for the star cat of the house*
Atlas *In Greek mythology, Atlas carried the world on his shoulders*
Attila *King of the Huns*
Audacity *Courage, boldness, daring*
Augustus *Nobility, high rank, as the ruler Caesar Augustus*
Aussie *Nickname for an Australian native*
Austin *Revered individual, short for Augustine*
Avalanche *Cascade of snow, good name for a white cat*
Avalon *Mythical paradise island in King Arthur's time*
Avery *Strong and powerful*
Axel *Reward, source of life*

Bacardi *A brand of rum*
Bailey *An Irish liqueur*
Baldric *Valiant and courageous, fearless prince, ruler*
Ballyhoo *Noisy uproar, loud talk*
Bambino *Italian for "baby"*
Bandit *Mischievous and into trouble*
Baron *A rank of nobility*
Basil *Majestic, also Bazil*

Beamer *Great name for a fancy cat, after the luxury car (BMW)*
Beau (Bo) *Very handsome, dashing*
Beauregard *French for "good-looking"*
Ben *Beloved son, short for Benjamin, Benny*
Benson *Gentle, mild mannered, well behaved*
Bentley *A flashy, classy, elegant cat*
Bing Clawsby *Bing Crosby play on words*
Blackberry *A sweet, black cat*
Blackie *An all black, or mostly black cat, also Black*
Blackjack *A playful black cat that loves games*
Blade *Dashing young male*
Blaze *Fire, a cat with a white blaze on its face*

SIR LIONEL—A FELINE ARISTOCRAT

We had decided on a Maine Coon. These majestic cats are "the greatest" not only in terms of weight, but also in their demeanor. Our little lion treated us condescendingly at first and with extreme caution. Because he radiated such an air of dignity, we gave him the name Sir Lionel, because he was lionlike and the title "Sir" seemed appropriate for him.

Blitz *Burst of lightning, energetic cat*
Blizzard *A heavy snowstorm, a white cat*
Blooper *A funny mistake, good name for a comical cat*
Blue *For the cat with a silvery blue coat color*
Bobby *Meaning "a great reputation," short for Robert, also Bob*
Bogart *Movie hero Humphrey Bogart, also Bogie*
Bonkers *Crazy and wild, nuts*
Bonzer *Australian for "excellent, attractive, pleasing"*
Boomer *Strong, bold, outgoing, always returns home, also Boomerang*
Boots *High white socks, or markings, on the hind feet*
Bourbon *A whiskey, name for a cat with rich brown coloration*

Brando *Actor Marlon Brando*
Brass *For a shiny, brass-colored cat, short for "the brass ring," high ranking*
Bubba *Slang for "buddy," or "friend"*
Buddy *A close friend and companion*
Buzz *The busybody cat*

Cadbury *Chocolate company in England*
Caesar *Ruler of the Roman Empire*
Cairo *Capital of Egypt*
Cappuccino *Italian espresso with milk*
Caramelo *Spanish for "caramel"*
Caruso *Italian opera singer*
Casanova *Italian adventurer, loved by women*
Casey *Baseball player in poem by E. L. Thayer*
Cassidy *Cowboy hero Hopalong Cassidy*

Catzilla *The cat in the movie Mouse Hunt*
Chaos *Greek for "extreme disorder and confusion"*
Charcoal *Very dark gray or brown, almost black*
Charles *Of French origin, also Charlie or Charley*
Chase *To hunt or follow quickly, for the cat that loves to hunt*
Cheshire *The Cheshire Cat in Alice in Wonderland*
Chico *"Boy" in Spanish*
Chief *Leader of a tribe*
Chopin *Famous pianist*
Cicero *Roman statesman and philosopher*
Cisco *After the bandit The Cisco Kid*
Clyde *Thief, from Bonnie and Clyde*
Coco *For a chocolate-colored cat*
Cognac *A French brandy distilled from wine*
Colombo *Droll detective from the TV series Colombo*
Columbus *Christopher Columbus*
Comet *A heavenly body with a tail*
Copper *Ideal for a reddish brown cat*
Cosmo *Pertaining to the heavens or cosmos*
Cousteau *Famous underwater diver Jacques Cousteau*
Crackers *Crazy, insane, nutty*
Cupid *God of love in Roman mythology, winged cherub*
Czar *King, ruler, also Tsar*

Cute **Names** for **Black** Tomcats

Have you lost your heart to a deep-black pussycat and found yourself looking for a suitable name? Here is a small assortment for your little devil or possibly even your cuddle cat: Blackberry, Blackie, Blackjack, Black Magic, Black Pearl, Charcoal, Coco, Darkstar, Ebony, Fudge, Hershey, Inky, Midnight, Onyx, Othello, Zip.

THE CRAZY SIAMESE TOM

He is the born clown in my community of felines. Even when he was quite young, he poked his little nose into everything that seemed edible to him, and of course into things that were none of his business. His best trick is jumping into the open refrigerator. The coveted turkey breast is stored there, and my kitty is well aware of that. Because he is truly so crazy, I named him Crazy.

Daiquiri *A cocktail*
Dakota *Meaning "ally" or "friend," a group of Native American tribes, also Sioux*
Dandy *First-rate and very good, also Dandelion*
Dante *Italian poet*
Dapple *Variegation of spots, mottles, or colors*
Darby *A devoted individual, from the 18th century English verse "Darby and Joan"*
Darcy *Australian champion boxer James Darcy*
Darkstar *Good name for a dark cat*
D'Artagnan *One of the three musketeers*
Darwin *British naturalist and writer*
Da Vinci *Italian artist*
Dazzler *A cat that arouses admiration with its brilliant qualities*

Dealer *A gambling cat that takes chances*
Derrick *English name meaning "mighty," "powerful"*
Descartes *Philosopher*
Diablo *Spanish for "devil"*

Diamond *A precious stone, a precious cat*
Dillinger *One of writer Ernest Hemingway's cats*
Dinky *The cat nephew of Felix in the comic series* Felix the Cat
Dino *Short for "dinosaur"*
Dionysus *Greek mythology god of wine and revelry*
Dixie *Jazz*
Domino *A cat with white spots*
Double Dare *Great name for the cat that takes chances*
Double Trouble *The name says it all*
Dreamweaver *Creator of dreams, also Dreamer for short*
Duke *A nobleman or prince*
Dumpling *Term of endear-ment*
Duncan *Scottish king*
Dustin *Meaning "courage," actor Dustin Hoffman*
Dusty *For a dust-colored cat*
Dylan *Singer and songwriter Bob Dylan*

Earl Grey *An English tea, great name for a gray cat*
Ebony *Deep, dark black wood*
Eclipse *Famous, outshining and overshadowing*
Ecstasy *One of writer Ernest Hemingway's cats*
Eddie *Nickname for Edward, meaning "guardian," "protector"*
Edsel *An outmoded model Ford car*
Einstein *Genius, scientist Albert Einstein, for a smart cat*
Elf *A tiny, prankish fairy*
Elite *The finest and most highly regarded*

Elmo *Fuzzy character on the TV show* The Muppets
Elton *Rock singer Elton John*
Elvis *Famous rock star Elvis Presley*
Emerson *Poet Ralph Waldo Emerson, classy name*
Emery *King or ruler*
Emperor *Ruler, king*
Enrico *Italian for Henry, meaning "powerful"*
Eric *Scandinavian name meaning "honor"*
Erin *Poetic name for Ireland*
Ernie *Short for Ernest, German word origin for "resolute"*
Eros *Greek god of love*
Errol *English name meaning "free man"*
ESP *Extrasensory perception*
Espresso *Italian coffee*
Esprit *French for "spirit"*
E.T. *Extra-terrestrial, from the movie* E.T.
Eugene *Greek name meaning "well born," also Gene*
Euripides *Greek writer of tragedies*

Fabian *Latin for "first" or "beginning"*
Felix *Latin for "happy," also the animated cartoon* Felix the Cat
Fernando *Italian for Ferdinand*
Ferrari *A fast, Italian sports car*
Fiasco *A blunder, ambitious project with a ridiculous ending*
Fiat *A fast, sporty cat, named after an Italian sports car*

Imaginative **Names** for **Twosomes**

Two males: Abbott and Costello, Batman and Robin, Fred and Barney, Penn and Teller, Peter and Paul, Tom and Jerry.
Mixed pairs: Adam and Eve, Bonnie and Clyde, Caesar and Cleopatra, Fred and Ethel, Romeo and Juliet, Tristan and Isolde, Yin and Yang.
Two females: Anna and Bella, Lisa and Marie, Mary and Lou, Snow White and Rose Red.

Figaro *Minnie Mouse's cat in the Disney animated cartoons*
Firecracker *A cat that loves to surprise*
Flambeau *French for a "lighted torch" or "large candlestick"*
Flame *Flickering fire, also a sweetheart*
Flash *A burst or blaze of light*
Florian *Latin for "decoration"*
Fluffy *The cat on the TV series* The Brady Bunch
Flynn *Masculine Irish name, actor Errol Flynn*
Folly *Foolishness*
Fondue *Cat on children's Nickelodeon TV series Kablam!*
Foul Play *A name for a cat that breaks the rules, alternate spelling Fowl Play*
Fox *A clever animal, reddish in color*
Francis *The patron saint of animals*
Freckles *For a cat with small, brownish spots*

Freddy *Short for Frederick, meaning "powerful"*
Freeze Frame *Scene taken from a motion picture to look like a photograph, dramatic effect, good for an active cat*
Friday *A faithful helper, the devoted servant of Robinson Crusoe*
Fritz *German masculine name, a famous cartoon cat*
Frost *For a white cat, after the frozen mist, crystalline coating*
Fudge *A sweet, dark cat*
Furball *For the very hairy cat*
Fuzzy *For the cat that is covered with soft, fine hairs*

Gable *Actor Clark Gable*
Gabriel *An angel, bearer of good news*
Gagarin *Russian cosmonaut*
Galahad *A pure and noble knight from the King Arthur legend*

Galileo *Italian mathematician, astronomer*
Gambler *One who plays games and takes chances for sport*
Ganymede *In Greek mythology, beautiful youth that was cupbearer for the gods*
Garfield *Cat in the comic-strip series* Garfield
Garnet *Crystal-like gem found in a variety of red colors*
Garth *Country-western singer* Garth Brooks
Gato *Spanish for "cat"*
Gatsby *The character in* The Great Gatsby *by F. Scott Fitzgerald*
Gavin *English name meaning "falcon"*
Gelato *Italian ice cream*
Genie *A genius, a supernatural form that grants wishes*
George *Meaning "earth worker," variations Georges, Jorge, Georgie*
Gershwin *American composer and pianist*
Ghirardelli *Dark chocolate-colored cat*

Gift *A present*
Gilligan *Shipwrecked character on the TV series* Gilligan's Island
Giovanni *Italian for Joe*
Gizmo *A gadget or a gimmick*
Glitter *Ideal name for a flashy, attractive cat*
Gobi *A vast desert in Mongolia*
Godot *From Samuel Beckett's* Waiting for Godot
Gourmand *For the cat that likes to overindulge*

Graffiti *For a cat with unusual markings, like scribbles on walls*
Grandiose *Grandeur and magnificence*
Gray *A masculine name, good for a gray cat*
Grog *A drink with rum, also* Groggy
Groucho *One of the Marx Brothers comedy team*
Guinness *Irish dark beer*
Gulliver *Main character in the political satire* Gulliver's Travels *by Jonathan Swift*
Gumshoe *A sneaky, stealthy detective*
Guru *A spiritual adviser*
Gus *Short for Angus or Augustus*

Hairy *As in Harry, for a very hairy cat, also* Harrison
Half-pint *Very small cat*
Hallmark *Genuine mark, stamped in gold or silver, high quality*
Hamlet *The main character in Shakespeare's* Hamlet

Names for the Zodiac Signs
Aries, Taurus, Gemini

Aries male: Al Capone, Carlo, Felix, Jimmy, Lincoln, Merlin, Ramses.
Aries female: Aisha, Caprice, Gracia, Kim, Lucy, Serafina, Shirley, Valeria, Vivian.
Taurus male: Adrian, Benny, Elvis, Florian, Garfield, Lazy, Pepper, Shadow, Yogi.
Taurus female: Evita, Farrah, Gina, Grenadine, Lulu, Sally, Scarlett, Tamara.
Gemini male: Dali, Leonardo, Misha, Prince, Sammy.
Gemini female: Amanda, Helen, Jade, Karma, Lollipop, Marilyn, Nina, Sheila.

Hannibal *General who crossed the Alps to invade Italy in 218 B.C.*
Hansel *From the children's fairy tale "Hansel and Gretel"*
Happy *For the contented cat*
Harlequin *Many colors, also a comic pantomime*
Harley *Harley Davidson, the popular motorcycle*
Harpo *The silent member of the Marx Brothers comedy team*
Hawkeye *For a cat with keen eyesight*
Hemlock *A poisonous plant*
Hercules *In mythology, the incredibly strong son of Zeus*
Hermes *Greek mythology god of science, he was messenger to other gods*
Hero *For the family pet hero, Greek for "watch over and protect"*
Hershey *A sweet, chocolate-colored cat, brand of chocolates*
Higgins *The professor in the movie* My Fair Lady
Holmes *Detective Sherlock Holmes in the story by A. C. Doyle*
Homer *Greek writer, author of* The Iliad *and* The Odyssey

Hooligan *A hoodlum or troublemaker*
Hoover *A good name for the cat that eats its food quickly*
Hopalong *Cowboy hero Hopalong Cassidy*
Hopkins *Actor Sir Anthony Hopkins*
Hot Rod *Speedy cat, a stripped car rebuilt for speed*
Houdini *Escape artist magician*
Hugo *Meaning "reason and intellect," author Victor Hugo*
Hugs *A huggable cat*
Humdinger *Slang for something excellent or special*

Hummer *For the oversized cat, named after the oversized jeep-like vehicle*
Hunter *Good name for a cat that loves to hunt*
Hurricane *A storm, violent tropical cyclone*

Icon *For the ultimate cat, an important individual, an image*
Iggy *A fun, nonsense, short name*
Igloo *A white cat or an Eskimo breed, after the Eskimo hut built of blocks of ice*
Igor *Russian masculine name*
Indiana Jones *Adventurer, hero, professor, and archaeologist in the Indiana Jones movies*
Indigo *Deep dark blue, one of seven colors in the rainbow*
Ingo *German mythology god Ingwio*
Inky *Darkly colored*

THAT'S KING

Nobody wanted him. We took the little cat home with us. Would he get along with Agatha, our elderly female cat? Agatha greeted him by hissing. But the little fellow didn't let himself be intimidated. With his head held high and his tail in the air, he simply marched right past Agatha. So we named him King, and because he was still so tiny we called him Little King.

Good **Names** for **Princes** and **Princesses**

They have a strong will. What they want, they get. Their humans subordinate themselves to them unconditionally. Here is a selection of suitable names.

Male: Admiral, Augustus, Baron, Caesar, Chief, Czar, Earl, Emperor, King, Napoleon, Prince.

Female: Anastasia, Baroness, Countess, Diva, Donna, Elmira, Milady, Prima Donna, Princess, Queen, Sabrina.

IQ *Intelligence quotient, level of intelligence*
Isidor *Greek for "gift," Izzy for short*
Ivan *Russian for John, first czar of Russia, Ivan the Terrible*

Jabberwocky *A nonsense poem of gibberish by Lewis Carroll*
Jackpot *A real winner cat, the highest stakes and winnings*
Jaguar *A sports car, also a large, fast feline*
Jason *Means "healer," in Greek mythology the prince who led the Argonauts and found the Golden Fleece*
Jasper *A precious cat named after the green precious stone, also a reddish, yellowish, or brownish quartz*
Jet *For a very fast, or very dark cat*
Jingles *A happy cat, light, ringing sounds, like bells*
Jinx *Mr. Jinx, the cat from the animated cartoon series, who*

chases mice Pixie and Dixie and says, "I hate meeces to pieces"
Joker *A cat that has a sense of humor*
Jolly *High spirits and good humor, happy*
Jones *Jones the cat was the only survivor (besides Ripley) in the movie* Alien, *also Jonesy*
Jordache *Fashion designer*
Jupiter *The god of all gods in Roman mythology, also the largest planet in our solar system*

K. C. *Short for Casey, Kasey*
Kasimir *Slavic name meaning "peacemaker"*
Katnip *From "Herman and Katnip," animated cartoon of the* Baby Huey Show
Kermit *The frog on the TV show* Sesame Street
King *Ruler, royalty, Disney movie* The Lion King
Kirby *Irish name, also Kerby*

Kirk *Captain Kirk of the TV series* Star Trek
Kiwi *A native of New Zealand, also a small, flightless bird*
Knickknack *A small, decorative ornament*
Knight *A servant of the king of high military rank*
Kodiak *For a giant, strong cat, after the large Alaskan bear*
Konrad *Meaning "bold," "counselor," "giver of advice"*
Kooky *Silly, ridiculous, eccentric*
Korbel *A cat with extravagant tastes, a brand of champagne*
Kudos *Praise, fame, admiration, glory*
Kumquat *Small orange fruit, ideal name for an Asian-breed cat*

Lafayette *Marquis de Lafayette, French general who fought in the American Revolution with his friend President George Washington*
Lamborghini *An expensive and fast cat, expensive Italian sports car*
Lancelot *Knight of the Round Table in King Arthur's legend*
Langley *The computer nerd in the TV series* The X-Files
Legacy *Value handed down from an ancestor*
Legend *Story or myth lasting generations*
Lenny *Short for Leonard, meaning "strong as a lion"*
Leo *Meaning "lion," constellation, sign of the zodiac, short for Leon*

HOW YO-YO GOT HIS NAME

Do you know a cat that continually runs back and forth or has all four paws in the air when jumping up in an effort to catch its "prey"? No? Then you don't know anything about Yo-Yo. Naming him after the well-known game of dexterity was the only possible solution. His favorite toy is the feline fishing pole: a little mouse made of fur on a rubber cord that you move to and fro in front of him. Then Yo-Yo is in his element.

Leonardo *Famous actor Leonardo Di Caprio, Italian for Leonard*

Leopold *Emperor of the Roman Empire*

Lexy *Short, attractive name, from Lexicon, an ancient language*

Liaison *A link, a love affair*

Licorice *For a sweet black or red cat, after the candy*

Linus *Charlie Brown's friend in the comic strip* Peanuts *by Charles Schulz*

Lion *Large, powerful feline considered "king of the beasts"*

Livewire *Energetic individual, a wire carrying an electrical current*

Livingston *Scottish explorer in Africa found by Sir Henry Morton Stanley*

Loco *Spanish for "crazy" or "demented"*

Logan *The highest mountain range in Canada*

Loki *God of fires in Norwegian legend*

London *The capital of the United Kingdom*

Long Shot *A slight chance of winning, so rewards are greater in a bet*

Lucky *Having good fortune or bringing good luck*

Macavity *Character in Andrew Lloyd Webber's musical* Cats

Macbeth *Scottish tartan, also the character in Shakespeare's play* Macbeth

Magic *Mysterious illusions, spells, charms*

Mars *Roman mythology god of war, Marco in Spanish*

Maximus *Latin for "greatest," "biggest," also Maximillian or Max*

Mephisto *Diabolical, crafty, powerful*

Merlin *Legendary magician who helped King Arthur*

Merlot *A red wine*

Michelangelo *Famous sculptor, painter, and architect*

Milo *The hero cat in the movie* Milo and Otis

Mitch *English masculine name*

Molière *French dramatist, writer*

Moochie *The black cat in the comic strip* Mutts *by Patrick McDonnell*

Moonshine *Illegally distilled whiskey*

Morris *The big yellow cat on the TV cat food commercials*

Motley *Patches of many colors*

Mr. Noodles *Big striped cat in the comic strip* Mutts

Mulder *The brilliant FBI agent in the TV series* The X-Files

Nacho *Kitty with tacos in the TV commercials*

Nairobi *Capital of Kenya, in Africa*

Napoleon *Emperor of France and military leader*

Nelson *English Admiral*

Nemo *Captain Nemo in* 20,000 Leagues Under the Sea *by Jules Verne*

Neptune *God of the sea in Roman mythology*

Nibbles *Also Nibble, or Nibbler*

Nick *Victory, short for Nicholas*

Nimbus *The flying witches' broom in* Harry Potter

Nino *Italian nickname for Antonio*

Nip *Short for Nipper, one of the Beanie Babies cats*
Noah *Hebrew masculine name meaning "rest and comfort"*
Nobel *Famous, illustrious, great character*
Nomad *A wanderer, for the cat that likes to wander*
Norton *The Scottish fold tabby in the story* The Cat Who Went to Paris *by Peter Gethers*
Nugget *A chunk of gold, gold colored, precious*

Odin *Norse mythology, god of art*
Odysseus *Hero in Homer's epic story* The Odyssey
Oliver *From Disney's animated movie* Oliver and Company, *nickname Ollie*
Omega *From Greek, meaning "great"*
Omen *Something that foretells a future event*
Onyx *Having colored layers, an agate, semiprecious stone*
Oregano *Fragrant herb used in cooking*
Oreo *A popular black-and-white cookie*
Orion *In Roman mythology, a hunter that was placed in the heavens as a constellation, in spoof movie* Men in Black *the cat that had the "galaxy" around its neck*
Orpheus *Greek mythology poet-musician with magical powers*
Oscar *The Muppet character who lives in a trash can, an award*

Othello *Main character in the Shakespearean tragedy* Othello
Otis *The adventuresome pug in the movie* Milo and Otis

Pablo *Spanish for Paul, Paolo in Italian*
Paddy *Nickname for English name Patrick, meaning "nobility"*
Paint *A piebald or pinto pattern*
Paisano *Spanish for "comrade" or "friend"*

Pan *In Greek mythology, the god of fields, forests, and wild animals*
Panther *A big, black, wild feline*
Paris *In Greek legend, he abducted Helen of Troy and started the Trojan War*
Parzival *Legendary hero, also Percival, Percy*
Pavarotti *Italian opera singer*
Peanuts *Cartoon strip by Charles Schulz, Peanut for a small cat*
Pedro *Spanish for Peter*
Pee Wee *A tiny cat*

Good Names for Smarty and Softy Types

They do everything calmly and agreeably. They treat their humans with affection and tenderness. These names are especially well suited to these gentle creatures:
Males: Amigo, Amor, Avalon, Diamond, Dreamer, Dumpling, Sweetie, Toby.
Females: Goldie, Gwendolyn, Harmony, Honey, Luna, Melody, Penelope, Precious.

Pepe *Romantic skunk in cartoon series* Pepe le Pew
Pepper *Good name for a black cat*
Pharaoh *King of Egypt in ancient times*
Picasso *Spanish artist Pablo Picasso*
Pierre *French for Peter*
Plato *Brown-and-white kitten in musical* Cats *by Andrew Lloyd Webber*
Pocket *A kitten small enough to fit in a pocket*
Polo *Fashion label, also Venetian traveler Marco Polo*
Poseidon *God of the sea and horses in Greek mythology*
Poucival *Gray-and-white cat in musical* Cats *by Andrew Lloyd Webber*
Pounce *Brown Beanie Babies cat*
Prance *Gray Beanie Babies cat with black stripes*
Prince *Royalty, handsome, future king*
Puck *Character from Shakespeare's* A Midsummer Night's Dream
Puff *Dick and Jane's cat in the book* Fun with Dick and Jane

Quincy *English name, composer Quincy Jones*
Quinn *Actor Anthony Quinn*
Quirinus *Roman mythology god of war*
Quixote *Don Quixote, the idealist in the story by Miguel de Cervantes*
Quo Vadis *Latin meaning "where are you going?"*

Radar *A cat that locates and follows*
Ramses *Egyptian Pharaoh*
Rebel *For the cat that resists authority*

Rembrandt *Dutch artist and painter*
Remington *Remington Steele, also Remy*
Remus *In Roman mythology, the twin brother of Romulus, nursed by a wolf*
Rex *Latin for "king"*
Rhett *Rhett Butler, dashing character in Margaret Mitchell's* Gone with the Wind
Riley *Valiant, also Reilly and O'Riley*
Ringleader *A leader, also a clownish troublemaker*
Ripley *Means "from the echo valley," good name for a cat that is hard to believe, Ripley's Believe It or Not museum*
Romeo *From Shakespeare's* Romeo and Juliet
Romulus *In Roman mythology, the first king of Rome and twin brother of Remus, both nursed by a wolf*

DR. DOOLITTLE, THE DIPLOMAT

He was the third member of our community of cats. Would the three get along well?, we wondered. But the little tom proved to be extremely diplomatic. He never annoyed the "old ones" beyond acceptable limits. He quickly became everyone's favorite. Even with our neighbors' dwarf rabbits, he was soon as thick as thieves. Because he obviously understood even the language of other animals, we named him Dr. Doolittle.

Rossini *Means "noble" and "proud," also composer Rossini*
Rufus *Meaning "red hair," in Spanish Rojo*
Rusty *Ellie Mae's swimming cat in the TV series* The Beverly Hillbillies

Salem *Black cat on TV series* Sabrina the Teenage Witch
Sampson *For the cat with a lot of hair, also Sammy, Sam*
Scamp *Mischievous rascal*
Scat Cat *Cat leader of the jazz band in Disney's animation* The Aristocats
Scooter *English name, a crazy cat*
Scotty *Good name for a Scottish fold cat, Scotty from* Star Trek
Scout *For an investigative cat*
Seuss *Dr. Seuss, author of* The Cat in the Hat
Shadow *A cat that follows everywhere*
Shakespeare *England's greatest playwright, William Shakespeare*
Shamrock *A good-luck cat*
Sherlock *Sherlock Holmes, famous detective*
Si *One of two Siamese cats in Disney's* Lady and the Tramp
Silver *Ideal name for a silvery cat*
Simba *Lion in Disney's animation* The Lion King
Sky *For a bluish gray cat, short for Skylar*
Smokey *Smoke color, grayish black, also Smoky*
Socks *A cat with white socks, also Soccer*

Names for Zodiac Signs
Cancer, Leo, Virgo

Cancer male: Alex, Andy, Buddy, Elton, Pepper.
Cancer female: Bella, Daisy, Mona, Phoebe, Raya.
Leo male: Kimba, Lion, Lionel, Nero, Simba.
Leo female: Artemis, Audrey, Dandelion, Huntress, Octavia.
Virgo male: Benson, Eros, Fernando, Rico.
Virgo female: Celina, Charm, Irina, Luna, Momo, Roxanne.

Socrates *Greek philosopher*
Soot *A black or dark cat*
Spartacus *Roman gladiator*
Spock *Mr. Spock, character on TV series* Star Trek
Spook *A member of Top Cat's gang in the Hanna-Barbera cartoon series* Top Cat
Sylvester *Black-and-white cat in the animated Loony Toons cartoons*

Tango *South American dance*
Teddy *Short for Edward, meaning "guardian," also a cuddly teddy bear*
Thor *Norse mythology, the god of thunder and strength*
Tigger *The tiger in* Winnie the Pooh *by A. A. Milne*
Titan *Great size, strength, power*
Tobermory *The talking cat in* The Chronicles of Clovis *by Saki*
Toby *Short for Tobias, meaning "precious"*
Tom *The tomcat in the animated cartoon series* Tom and Jerry

Tonto *Harry's orange tabby cat in the movie* Harry and Tonto
Toonces *The cat who could drive a car, on* Saturday Night Live
Top Cat *Leader of a gang of cats on the Hanna-Barbera cartoon series* Top Cat
Toulouse *The brown kitten in Disney's animation* The Aristocats
Tracker *A hunting cat*
Trapper *A hunting cat*
Trouble *A name for the cat that is often in trouble, also Troubles*
Turbo *Fast, powerful, supercharged*

Ulysses *Same as Odysseus, the hero in Homer's* The Odyssey
Umberto *Italian for Humbert, meaning "young bear"*
Unikat *A unique cat*
Uranus *Greek god of the heavens*

Uri *Uri Geller the psychic*
Ustinov *Actor Peter Ustinov*
Utrillo *French painter
Maurice Utrillo*

Vader *Darth Vader from the
movie* Star Wars
Valentine *Sweetheart*
Van Gogh *Famous painter*
Verdi *Italian opera composer*
Viking *Scandinavian sea
rover, pirate*
Vivaldi *Italian violinist and
composer*
Voltaire *French philosopher
and writer*

Waldo *Means "ruler," also
"Where's Waldo?" game*
Wallace *Alfred Russel
Wallace, naturalist, also Wally*
Watson *Friend of detective
Sherlock Holmes*
Webster *The large black cat
in* The Story of Webster *by P.
J. Wodehouse*
Whirligig *A toy that moves in
circles*
Whiskers *A fun name for a
lovable cat*
Whiskey *Strong alcoholic liquor*
Whisper *A quiet cat*

Widget *A hypothetical gadget*
William *The adventuresome cat
in* The Cat in the Lifeboat *by
James Thurber, nickname Willie*
Windsor *Windsor Castle,
home of British royalty*
Wolfgang *Composer Wolfgang
Amadeus Mozart*
Won Ton *A Chinese dumpling,
good name for Asian breed*

Xaver *A castle in Spain*
Xeno *Greek for "foreigner" or
"stranger"*
Xerxes *A Persian king*

Yankee *Native of the United
States, also Yankee Doodle*
Yeti *The abominable snow-
man in the Himalayas, great
name for a big white cat*

Yodel *A style of singing popular among mountain people
in the Alps*
Yogi *Animated cartoon character Yogi Bear*
Yosemite *A national park in
the United States*
Yo-yo *An active and eccentric cat*
Yukon *Territory in Canada*

Zachariah *Means "remem-
bered," also Zac, Zack, or Zak
for short*
Zappa *Rock music star Frank
Zappa*
Zeus *Ruler of the gods in
Greek mythology*
Zip *The black Beanie Babies cat*
Zola *French novelist Emile Zola*
Zorro *Legendary masked hero,
Spanish for "fox"*

Good Names
for Lovable Adventurers

These cats are open to all kinds of new things. Life can never offer enough variety
for them. They even like unfamiliar visitors—and that is saying a lot where cats are
concerned. Here are some suitable names for these little "wild things":
Males: Acrobat, Barney, Casanova, Columbus, D'Artagnan, Errol, Ferrari, Gulliver,
Legend, Nemo.
Females: Amelia, Carla, Fanny, Feisty, Gypsy, Liz, Pepsi, Razzmatazz, Stardust, Wanda.

The Best Names
for Females

Abigail *Means "father rejoices," also Abby for short*
Adriana *Latin meaning "from Adria," an Italian city*
Aida *Romantic, extravagant, Verdi's opera* Aida
Aimée *French meaning "beloved one," also Amy*
Aja *From Italian meaning "educated," for the smart cat*
Akira *Japanese for "intelligent and bright"*
Alabaster *Greek for "vessel of the goddess," ideal for a white cat*
Alaska *Ideal name for a snowy white cat*
Alba *Latin for "white"*
Alexa *World traveler and worldly wise, short for Alexandria*
Alice *Meaning "truth," also main character in* Alice in Wonderland *by Lewis Carroll, also Alicia*
Amalia *Meaning "courage," French variation Amélie*
Amanda *Latin for "worthy of love," Mandy or Mandi for short*
Amber *A deep amber color*
Amelia *Very feminine, yet adventurous*

Fine-sounding Names for White Beauties

They are absolutely beautiful, with their white coats. When something is so special, a special name is called for. Here are some possibilities for your pretty puss: Alabaster, Alaska, Alba, Arctica, Blanche, Crystal, Diamond, Ice Cream, Ice Queen, Pearl, Snowball, Snowflake, Snow Queen, Snow White, Vanilla, White, Whitney.

Amiga *Spanish for "good friend and companion"*
Anastasia *Perfect for the feline princess*
Angel *Always good, kind, lovable, perfectly well behaved*
Angelina *Another form of Angel, also Angela, Angie*
Anika *Russian for Annie*
Anna, Annie *Meaning "grace"*
Annabell, Anabella, Anabel *Combination of Ann and Belle*
Aphrodite *Goddess of love in Greek mythology*
Apricot *Excellent name for a sweet, light orange cat*

April *Ideal for a cat born in the springtime or month of April*
Aria *Vocal solo in an opera*
Ariel *The airy spirit in Shakespeare's* The Tempest
Aries *A constellation, the first sign of the zodiac*
Arpège *Fancy perfume*
Artemis *Greek goddess of hunting and the animal kingdom*
Asina *Nordic name for "goddess"*
Astra *Like a star*
Athena *Greek goddess of wisdom and art*

Audrey *Strong and noble*
Aurelia *Latin for "sweet one"*
Aurora *Roman goddess of new dawn, red morning sky*
Autumn *Born in the fall, or colored shades of autumn*
Azalea *A plant that produces numerous, colorful flowers*

Babette *French name, endearment*
Beauty *Extremely attractive, beautiful*
Bebe *Very small, also French for "baby"*
Belladonna *A beautiful lady, also a poisonous plant*
Belle *French for "very pretty," also Bella*
Bianca *White or very light colored*
Bibi *Short for Barbara*
Bijou *French for "jewel"*
Bitsy *Something small, itsy bitsy*
Bliss *Happiness, joy*

Blithe *Cheerful, carefree, gleaming*
Blondie *Blonde colored, also a rock singer from the 1980s*
Blossom *Flowers, buds, and blooms in a cluster*
Bonbon *A French candy*
Bonita *Spanish for "very pretty"*
Bordeaux *An excellent wine from the Bordeaux region of France*
Brandy *A liquor, a deep, dark, golden color*
Brazen *Copper in color, bold*
Breezy *Light, airy, like the breeze*
Brit *Celtic word meaning "speckled, varicolored"*
Brittany *Region in France, Britt for short*
Brownie *Good name for a sweet, dark, chocolate-colored cat*
Bubbles *A bubbly personality, lively, happy*
Buff *A pale color, also Buffy*

Bunny *Baby rabbit, good name for a small, cuddly cat*
Burgundy *Deep purplish color, region of France famous for wines*
Buttercup *Bright yellow flower*
Butterscotch *A light yellow-brown mixture of brown sugar and butter, perfect name for a butterscotch-colored cat with a sweet personality*
Buttons *An ideal name for a small, bright, lively cat*

Calypso *The sea nymph who kept Odysseus on her island in Homer's* The Odyssey
Camille *French name for "integrity and perfect character"*
Candy *A sweet treat*
Caper *Playful, frisky, skip, leap*
Caprice *Sudden change in behavior according to whim*
Caramel *Sweet name for a brown or honey-colored cat*
Carmen *Seductive main character in Bizet's opera* Carmen
Chablis *A white wine, origi-nally from Chablis, France*
Champagne *A white wine regarded as a symbol of luxury*
Chantilly *A type of lace, origi-nally from Chantilly, France*
Charade *A game acted out in pantomime, great for a playful cat*
Charisma *Means "gift of grace," beauty, kindness*
Charm *Perfect for an enchant-ing, attractive, magical cat*

Good **Names** for the **Eternal Child**

These cats are ready for any kind of mischief, and they remain quite playful even in old age. They love feeling safe and secure. These names are appropriate for them:
Males: Alf, Crazy, Felix, Gift, Happy, Harlequin, Jingles, Joker, Jolly, Livewire.
Females: Angel, Aurelia, Bibi, Candy, Darling, Happiness, Kiki, Kitty, Marshmallow, Serena.

SNOWPAWS

It was a bitterly cold winter night. We were sitting in the living room around the cozy, warm fireplace. Suddenly something outside scratched at the terrace door. I quickly opened it. Its four paws covered with snow, a kitten wobbled into the room. And that's how Snowpaws got her name. Since that time our darling wants nothing to do with the white splendor of nature. Go outdoors when snow is on the ground? Nothing doing, not for Snowpaws.

Chelsea *Popular feminine name, a borough of London*
Chère *French for "dear," also Cherie, Cher*
Chica *Spanish for "little girl"*
Chiffon *Light, fancy, sweet, as in chiffon lace or chiffon pie*
Cinder *Short for Cinderella, a good name for a dark-colored cat*
Cinnamon *A spice used for desserts, fun name for a yellowish brown cat*
Cleo *Short for Cleopatra*
Cloudy *Great name for a cat with patches of white in the coat*
Cocopuff *A chocolate-colored, fluffy cat, also Cocoa*
Confetti *Little bits of colored candy or paper, for the cat with a sweet yet colorful personality*

Cookie *A clever cat, as in "a smart cookie," slang for an attractive female*
Coquette *A flirt*
Crumpet *A little cake*
Crystal *Clear and brilliant, pure*
Cupcake *A sweet little cake, term of endearment*

Dabble *Good name for the unusual cat that likes to play in water*
Daisy *A flower, also Donald Duck's girlfriend*
Dancer *Moves lightly, prances*
Dandelion *French dent de lion meaning "tooth of a lion," a flower*
Daphne *A nymph in Greek mythology who escaped from Apollo*
Darcy *Short, attractive, feminine name, variation Darcie*
Darling *Something very dear, cherished, and loved, also Darla*
Dawn *Early morning, the famous blue-merle collie in Albert Payson Terhune's story Gray Dawn*
Dee Dee *A nickname, also short for Diane or Diana*
Delia *Feminine form of Delios, also an island in the Aegean Sea*
Destiny *Fate, intended purpose, from French destinée*
Diamond *A precious gem*
Dice *For a white cat with black spots*
Dido *Mischievous prank or caper, New Age singer*
Diva *Prima donna, leading female singer in an opera*
Dolly *Nickname for Dorothy, young, pretty, lovable*
Duchess *Nobility and rank, also Duchesse*

35

Echo *Reflection of sound*
Éclair *An oblong French pastry filled with cream, also Claire*
Eden *A wonderful place or garden*
Edelweiss *Small, white flower as in the song "Edelweiss"*
Ella *Nickname for Eleanor, also Ellie*
Elmira *Arabic for "princess"*
Elsie *Derived from Alice or Elizabeth, also Elsa*
Elvira *Spanish feminine name*
Elysian *Happy, delightful, blissful*
Ember *For a cat with a glowing personality*
Emily *Feminine name for Emil, Roman origin*
Emma *Emma Peel, the fictitious secret agent, also Emmy*
Enya *New age singer Enya*
Esmeralda *The young woman in Victor Hugo's story* The Hunchback of Notre Dame
Estella *Italian for "star," Estrella in Spanish*
Eunice *A good victory, of Greek origin*

Fabergé *A brand of perfume*
Faith *Feminine name, belief, trust, confidence*
Fanny *Feminine nickname for Frances, French word origin*
Fantasia *A musical composition, also Disney's movie*
Fawn *Good name for a pale yellowish brown cat*
Feather *Soft, lightweight, feathery*

Good **Names** for Sensitive **Creatures**

To gain the confidence of these hypersensitive little creatures, it takes tact, understanding, and patience. The following names are appropriate for these shy souls:
Males: Bo, Cicero, Dante, Ganymede, Homer, Licorice, Valentine, Vivaldi.
Females: Cara, Cupcake, Kiss, Lea, Melinda, Shy, Sleeping Beauty.

Feisty *An energetic, lively cat full of spirit*
Fendi *Fashion design label*
Fiona *Gaelic for "pretty," "white"*
Firefly *A winged beetle active at night that glows*
Flair *A natural talent or ability, stylish, dashing*
Fleur *French for "flower"*
Flirt *To play at love*
Flora *In Roman mythology, the goddess of flowers*
Flossy *Like light and fluffy, stylish or fancy, also Flossie*
Flower *Flowers made of petals and stems, usually brightly colored*
Flutterby *A mix that sounds like "butterfly"*
Foxy *Clever, attractive, seductive, or reddish brown color*
Frostie *Frost, ice, cold and white, also Frosty*

Gabby *Short for Gabriella, named after the archangel Gabriel*
Gatta *Italian for "cat"*
Gem *A precious stone, also Gemma*
Georgia *Feminine for George, songs "Sweet Georgia Brown" and "Georgia," a southern state in the United States*
Gigi *Promise or pledge, short for Gilberta*
Gina *Italian feminine name, short for Gianna*
Gingersnap *A cookie made from ginger, good name for a golden, sassy cat that nips, nickname Ginger*
Giselle *From the romantic ballet* Giselle
Givenchy *Fashion designer*
Gloria *Great honor and praise, also Glory*
Godiva *Lady Godiva rode naked through Coventry to plead her case for lower taxes (about 1,000 years ago)*

Goldie *A golden color, short for Goldilocks of "Goldilocks and the Three Bears"*
Grace *Graceful, elegant, classy, also Gracie*
Graymalkin *Reference to a cat in Shakespeare's* MacBeth
Grenadine *A syrup made from pomegranates*
Greta *A pearl, short for Margaret, also Gretta and Gretchen*
Gretel *From the children's fairy tale "Hansel and Gretel"*
Griselda *From German, meaning "gray," also heroine*
Grizabella *The gray cat in the musical* Cats *that sings "Memory"*
Guinevere *The wife of King Arthur, means "white phantom"*

Gumdrop *A colorful chewy candy, good name for a small, colorful cat*
Gummie Bear *A chewy, sweet candy in various colors, shaped like little bears*
Gussie *Nickname for Augusta, also Gussy*
Gwendolyn *Old English feminine name*
Gypsy *Wandering fortune-teller, musician*

LA CHICA FROM THE COSTA BRAVA

The tiny little kitten had probably lost its mama. Alone and meowing pitifully, it showed up every evening on the terrace of the vacation home we had rented in Spain. Who can resist that? The kitten got only the best of foods and finally did not budge from our side. We named the kitty La Chica, as a true Spaniard—it means "little girl"—and took her home with us.

Halley *Halley's comet, also Haley*
Hanna *Short for Joanna, also Hannah, means "blossom"*
Happy *Content, carefree, pleased*
Harmony *Pleasant sounding tones in music*
Hazel *Great name for a cat with light yellow brown eyes or coat color*
Heather *A Scottish plant with bell-shaped, purple-pink flowers*
Helen *Helen of Troy, the beautiful queen whose abduction caused the Trojan War, also Helena*
Henna *For the cat with auburn hair*
Hilda *Short for German Brunhilda, also Hildy*
Hollywood *Home of movie studios and movie stars, variation Holly Would!, also Holly*
Honey *Cute name for a sweet honey-colored cat, one that "sticks" close by*
Hoopla *Excitement, bustle, ballyhoo*
Hope *Feminine name meaning "trust and reliance"*
Huntress *For the cat that loves to hunt*

Ice Queen *For a snowy white cat*
Ida *Old English for "prosperous"*
Iduna *Nordic goddess of eternal youth*
Inca *An Indian tribe from Peru*
India *Large region of southern Asia*

Indira *Indian name meaning to "sparkle" or "twinkle"*
Ingrid *Feminine Scandinavian name*
Inkling *Notion or suggestion, a vague idea*
Ink Spot *Good name for a cat with black spots*
Iota *Very small, a tiny bit, name for a very tiny cat*
Irene *In Greek mythology, the goddess of peace, also Irina*
Iris *In Greek mythology, the goddess of the rainbow*
Isabella *The Spanish queen who funded Columbus's voyage*
Isis *The Egyptian goddess of fertility*
Isolde *From the Opera* Tristan and Isolde *by Richard Wagner*
Ivory *White, precious material from the tusks of elephants*
Ivy *A trailing, climbing, decorative vine*

Jade *Green, a precious stone used for jewelry*
Jasmine *A tropical plant with fragrant flowers*
Jezebel *A tricky woman, play on words is Jazzabelle*

Jellybean *A sugary bean-shaped colorful candy, perfect name for a chubby, round cat*
Jemima *A cat from the musical* Cats
Jenny *A cat from the musical* Cats
Jewel *Precious, valuable, gem*
Jonquil *French for "daffodil" or narcissus flowering plant*
Josephine *Napoleon's wife, the French empress*
Joy *Happy, delightful, merry*

Jubilee *A celebration*
Juliet *The heroine in Shakespeare's* Romeo and Juliet

Kalila *Arabic for "beloved"*
Karen *Nordic name for Karin*
Karma *Fate, destiny*
Kassandra *In Greek mythology, Apollo gave Kassandra prophetic powers to try to win her love*
Katherine *Another spelling of Catherine*
Katie *Nickname for Catherine, also Kitty*
Katydid *For the cat that's always into trouble, a fun play on words is "Katy did!"*
Keepsake *Kept for the memories, special and precious*
Kelly *A feminine Irish name, Grace Kelly, princess of Monaco*
Kenya *A country in Africa*

LITTLE STAR—MY LITTLE DEVIL

Little Star's coat is pitch black. The only white is a star-shaped patch on the middle of her chest. That's where she got her name. She doesn't tolerate visitors at all. When company's present, she often reveals her devilish side. Recently my friend tried to tempt her with some cream. She licked it off his finger with pleasure, but then bit it as hard as she could. "Good bait catches fine fish," but not my Little Star.

Names for the Zodiac Signs
Libra, Scorpio, Sagittarius

Libra male: Angelo, Chester, Happy, Ringleader.
Libra female: Dolly, Ember, Mindy, Passion, Sugar.
Scorpio male: Bogart, D'Artagnan, Hamlet, Michelangelo.
Scorpio female: Alexa, Cleo, Nikita, Olympia.
Sagittarius male: Ashley, Romulus, Yankee, Zorro.
Sagittarius female: Diana, Molly, Pandora, Tigerlily, Venus.

Kerry *Short for Karen and Katherine, a county in Ireland*
Kiara *Simba's daughter in Disney's animated movie* The Lion King
Kiki *A fun, nonsense name*
Kimberly *A city in the Cape of Good Hope, also Kim*
Kiss *Sign of affection, love*
Kitkat *A candy name for a sweet cat, chocolate in color*
Kitty *Term of endearment, baby cat*
Kiwi *A native of New Zealand, a small green fruit, a flightless bird*
Klee *German for "clover," for a good-luck cat*

Lacey *Popular feminine name, a fine lace in ornamental designs*
Lady *For the cat with class*
Ladybug *A bright colored, tiny beetle*
Lambkin *Gentle, innocent, loved, term of endearment*

Lara *Short for Larissa or Laura*
Laura *Variation on Laurentius, feminine of Laurence*
Leah *Short, feminine name, also Lea, meaning "antelope"*
Leda *A Spartan queen in Greek mythology*
Liberty *Freedom*
Lillie Langtry *Popular English actress (1852–1929)*
Limoges *A fine porcelain from Limoges, France*
Lindsay *Old English name, also Lindsey*
Liz *Short for Elizabeth, also Lizzy or Lizzie*
Lola *Spanish, short for Dolores, also Lolita*
Lollipop *A candy sucker on a stick, also Lolli or Lolly*
Loretta *Pet name for Lora*
Lorna Doone *A cookie named after the romance novel by R. D. Blackmore*
Lotus *A water lily, a fruit that causes dreaminess*
Lovebug *Term of endearment, small flying bug*

Lucy *Nickname for Lucille, also Lucinda*
Lulu *Slang for a beautiful girl, short for Louise*
Luna *Roman goddess of the moon*
Lyra *Constellation in the northern sky*

Mabel *From Latin* amabilis, *meaning "lovable"*
Madeline *Variation of Magdalene, Greek feminine name*
Madonna *Female rock singer*
Maggie *Short for Margaret, also Maggy*
Maisy *English feminine name*
Maleah *Unique combination of May and Leah*
Maliblue *Play on words from Malibu, good for a silvery or bluish-colored cat*
Mandi *Short for the English name Amanda, also Mandy*
Marbles *Great name for a cat with a marbling pattern in its coat*
Margarita *A pearl, an alcoholic drink*
Margot *French for Margo*
Mariah *Song "They Call the Wind Mariah" from the Broadway hit* Paint Your Wagon
Marian *Robin Hood's lady friend*
Mariposa *Spanish for "butterfly"*
Marmalade *Cat in the TV series* The Beverly Hillbillies, *owned by Sam Drucker*

Marshmallow *The perfect name for a soft, white, sweet, cuddly cat*

Mata Hari *Famous exotic dancer accused of spying*

Maxine *Feminine name for Max*

May *Spring month, also short for Mary or Margaret, or Mae, as in Mae West*

Maya *Hindu goddess, an illusion*

Megan *Of Greek origin, meaning "great, mighty"*

Melanie *Ideal name for a black cat, from the Greek word meaning "black"*

Melinda *Tender, delicate*

Melody *A pleasing song*

Mercedes *Spanish feminine name, also a luxury car*

Merry *Happy, full of fun and laughter*

Mia *Famous soccer player Mia Hamm*

Mimi *Hello Kitty's twin sister in the cartoon series*

Mimosa *A genus of trees and plants with small, colorful flowers*

Mindy *Nickname, also short for Melinda*

Minette *Popular French name for cats*

Minnie *Very small or miniature, Mickey Mouse's girlfriend Minnie Mouse in the Disney animated cartoon series*

Missy *Endearment for "young miss," also Missie*

Mistral *Strong winds that blow over the Mediterranean coast of France*

Good Names for Sociable Felines

They don't like quarrels. Within the cat group, they settle disputes. A lack of harmony in any form is abhorrent to them. Suitable names:

Males: Amigo, Angelo, Blade, Cupid, Hugs, Jason, Merlin, Teddy.

Females: Agatha, Aimée, Angelina, Dolly, Faith, Hope, Merry, Prudence, Tiffany.

Misty *Fine vapor, as in a mist of perfume*

Mocha *Chocolate-flavored coffee, color of mocha*

Molasses *For a dark-colored, very sweet cat, or for a cat that is, according to the old expression, "as slow as molasses in winter"*

Molly *Nickname for Mary*

Mona *Means "noble," also Da Vinci's painting Mona Lisa*

Moonlight *Soft light of the moon*

Moonshadow *"I'm being followed by a moonshadow" lyrics from Cat Stevens song "Moonshadow"*

Moppet *Term of endearment, a rag doll*

Mosaic *Artwork made of bits and pieces of colors*

Ms. Demeanor *Play on words for "misdemeanor," not behaving*

Muffin *An affectionate name*

Mystery *Secret, difficult to explain*

Mystique *Mystical feelings surrounding an individual*

Nadja *Short for Russian feminine name Nadjescha*

Nala *Simba's friend in the Disney animated movie* The Lion King

Nanna *Nickname for Anna*

Nanette *French nickname for Nancy*

Naomi *Hebrew origin, meaning "my delight"*

Natalie *Nickname for French name Natalia*

Natasha *Russian nickname for Natalie, meaning "born on Christmas"*

Nelly *Combination of Helen and Eleanor*

Nightshade *Poisonous plant*

Nikita *Special agent in the film by Luc Besson*

Nina *Endearment, Spanish for "daughter"*
Noche *Spanish for "evening"*
Noisette *French for "hazelnut and chocolate"*
Nora *Short for Leonora or Eleonore*
Norma *A constellation in the Milky Way*
Nutter Butter *A name of a nutty, buttery cookie*
Nymph *Nature goddess*

Octavia *Latin for eighth child*
Odessa *Ukrainian port on the Black Sea*
Odette *French for Oda*
Olivia *Variation of Olive, Popeye's girlfriend*
Olympia *Feminine Greek name for site of Olympic Games*
Opal *Precious stone that reflects light in various colors*
Ophelia *Greek for "helper," the woman in love with Hamlet in Shakespeare's play Hamlet*

Orchid *Distinctive, brightly colored tropical flower*
Ornament *Decoration or embellishment*
Ostara *German mythology goddess of spring*

Paisley *An intricate pattern and design*
Pamela *Greek meaning "dark" or "black"*
Pandora *In Greek mythology, the first mortal woman*
Pansy *A bright flower*
Paola *Italian for Paula*
Papillon *French for "butterfly"*

Paprika *A powdered red pepper, good for a reddish-colored and sassy cat*
Passion *Deep emotion, a brand of perfume*
Pastel *Light, soft color*
Patch *A patch of color, also Patches*
Paula *Latin for "little one"*
Peaches *Endearment, sweet, loving*
Pearl *Precious rounded gem, ideal for black or white*
Penelope *Faithful wife of Odysseus in Homer's* The Odyssey, *also Penny*
Pepsi *Lively and energetic, a popular soft drink, for a cat with a bubbly personality*
Petunia *Colorful garden flower*
Phoebe *Goddess of the moon in Greek mythology*
Polly *Short for English name Apollonia*
Porsche *Expensive German sports car*
Precious *Beloved, dear, of great value*

Names for the Zodiac Signs
Capricorn, Aquarius, Pisces

Capricorn male: Hannibal, Hercules, Hugo, Konrad, Nathan, Orion, Thor.
Capricorn female: Amelia, Audrey, Gloria, Megan, Minerva, Natasha, Rikki, Victoria.
Aquarius male: Edison, Fellini, Gambler, Holmes, Houdini, Loco, Mephisto.
Aquarius female: Barbarella, Cher, Colette, Flirt, Gigi, Karma, Ophelia, Tracy.
Pisces male: Astro, Colin, Gulliver, Lolly, Smarty, Sweetie, Tango, Toby, Vivaldi.
Pisces female: Adriana, Astra, Bianca, Charisma, Destiny, Jodie, Lucy, Naomi.

Prima Donna *For the most special, top cat*
Princess *Royalty, the daughter of a queen*
Prudence *Feminine name from Latin, wise, discreet, careful*
Puma *A cougar, a large, wild feline*

QT *As in "cutie"*
Queen *Royalty, also Queenie*
Querida *Spanish for "beloved"*
Quiana *Indian name meaning "graceful, charming"*
Quiver *For the cat that moves around a lot*

Rainbow *Ideal for a colorful cat*
Raisin *A fun name for a small, sweet, dark cat. Play on words is Raison, as in* raison d'être *(French for "reason to be")*
Rapunzel *For the long-haired cat, after the girl with long, golden hair in Grimm's fairy tale* Rapunzel
Razzledazzle *Flashy, bewildering*
Razzmatazz *Lively excitement, also Razz*
Reba *Short for Rebecca, the captivator*
Renée *French for Renate, or "reborn," also Rena or Renata*
Revlon *A brand of cosmetics*
Rhonda *Beach Boys song "Help Me Rhonda"*
Rikki *Powerful ruler, feminine of Ricardo*

A REAL PRINCESS

Daintily, with silky coat and head raised high, she made her entrance into our home. She inspected the apartment graciously. She looked here and looked there, until she ended up in front of the closed bedroom door. A reproachful glance back at us, and we solicitously hurried to open it for her. Aha, something useful at last—the freshly made bed. And then she made herself comfortable on it. The only name for this cat is Princess.

Risa *Short for Amarisa*
Rosey *Beautiful, fragrant flower, also Rosie, Rosa*

Roxane *Cyrano's love in* Cyrano de Bergerac *by Rostand*
Ruby *Precious red gem*

Sabrina *Princess, teenage witch on the TV series* Sabrina the Teenage Witch
Sadie *A variation of Sarah*
Saffron *A very expensive, yellow spice, the perfect name for a yellowish cat*
Sahara *The world's largest desert, in North Africa*
Sally *A variation of Sarah*
Salsa *Latin American dance music, a hot dip*
Samantha *Feminine name for Samuel or Sam*
Sandy *For a cat that is light brown*
Saphira *Greek for "pretty"*
Sapphire *A blue gem, good name for a bluish or silvery cat*

Sarah *Meaning "royalty, princess"*
Sasha *Helper, also Sascha or Sacha*
Sassy *Lively and spirited, the cat in the movie* The Incredible Journey
Savanne *French for "savannah, grasslands"*
Scarlett *Scarlett O'Hara, main character in Margaret Mitchell's book* Gone with the Wind, *play on words "Scarlett O'Hairy"*
Scribbles *For a cat with interesting coat patterns or markings*
Scully *FBI agent in the TV series* The X-Files
Selene *Greek moon goddess, also Selena*
Señorita *Spanish for "miss"*
Serena *Tranquil, serene, variation Serina*
Shady Lady *A lady of secrecy and mystery*
Shakira *Arabic for "graceful, charming"*
Shana *Gift of grace*
Shannon *A river in Ireland*
Shasta *Sweet and bubbly, a mountain in California*
Sheba *Queen of Sheba, wealthy queen*
Sheila *Australian slang for "girl"*
Sherry *A dry wine*
Sienna *City in Italy, for a cat that is the color of clay earth*
Siren *In Greek mythology, a seductive sea nymph, also Sirena*

Smooch *Hug or kiss, lovable*
Smudge *Good for a dark cat or one with dark markings*
Snowball *Ideal for a white cat, also Snow, Snowy*
Sophie *Skill, wisdom, variation of Sophia*
Sparkle *An attractive cat with a bubbly personality*
Stardust *Enchanting, dreamlike, cluster of faraway stars, nickname Star*
Stella *Short for Estella, meaning stellar, starlike*
Sugar *Sweet, lovable, white cat*
Summer *For a cat born in the summertime*
Sushi *Ideal name for a cat that loves gourmet fish*
Sweet Pea *A flower, term of endearment, also Sweetie*
Sylvie *French for Sylvia*

Tabby *Gray or brown cat with dark stripes*
Tabitha *Greek for "gazelle," a fast animal*
Taffy *A chewy, sweet candy*
Taiga *The northern forests of Eurasia and North America*
Tamara *Hebrew word for "date palm," also Tammy, Tara*
Tanja *Short for Russian name Tatjana, also Tanya, Tonya*
Tasha *Short for Natasha*
Tequila *A Mexican alcoholic drink*
Tessa *Short for Theresa, also Tess, Tessie*
Theresa *Greek word meaning "harvester," nickname Tracy*
Tiara *A small crown or headdress*
Tiffany *Fancy New York jewelers, movie* Breakfast at Tiffany's

Suitable Names for Long-haired Cats

When their coats are groomed, the "longhairs" look fabulous. Therefore they should have names that do justice to their lush coats of hair.
Males: Adonis, Furball, Hairy, Leonardo, Samson, Sir Lionel, Teddy.
Females: Cocopuff, Daphne, Fay, Feather, Flossy, Godiva, Rags, Rapunzel, Taiga, Velvet.

Tigerlily *Character from James Barrie's story* Peter Pan, *also Tiger*

Tigress *A female tiger, sleek, ferocious*

Tilly *Nickname for Emily or Matilda*

Tina *Short for Christina*

Tinkerbell *The tiny fairy in James Barrie's story* Peter Pan

Tiny *A name for a very, very small cat*

Tippy *A short, fun name, also Tippie, or Tipsy*

Tonia *Short for Antonia, a name of Latin origin*

Tootsy *Term of endearment for a sweetheart*

Tori *Short for Victoria*

Tortie *For a tortoiseshell cat*

Tosca *Main character in Puccini's opera* Tosca

Trixie *Clever, lucky*

Truffles *For a sweet, chocolate-colored cat*

Turandot *Of Chinese origin, princess, from the opera by Puccini*

Tweetie *The little canary in Warner Brothers animated cartoons, Tweetie Pie*

Twiggy *Super-thin model, good for a slender breed*

Una *Latin for "unity, number one"*

Urania *In Greek mythology, the daughter of Zeus*

Ursula *Latin for she-bear, legendary British princess*

Ute *German feminine name, also Uta*

Nice **Names** for **Red Pussycats**

Red is trendy, and not only where women's hair color is concerned. Feline carrottops, too, are popular. These names make some reference to the coat color:

Males: Aspen, Ginger, Leroy, Robin, Roy, Rufus, Rusty.

Females: Amber, Aurora, Autumn, Chili, Lola, Paprika, Rose, Rosalie, Rosanna, Rose Red, Ruby, Zinfandel, Zora.

Utopia *An imaginary island, a perfect place*

Valentina *Feminine name for valentine, sweetheart*

Valeria *Latin origin meaning "to be strong," also Valerie, Val*

Valeska *Polish for Valeria*

Vanessa *Actress Vanessa Redgrave*

Vanilla *Name for a white cat, fragrant plant used in flavoring*

Velvet *For a soft cat, such as a Rex breed*

Venezia *A region of northern Italy*

Venus *Roman mythology goddess of love and beauty*

Vera *Truth, faith, word of Latin origin*

Verena *Latin for "honest and sincere"*

Veritas *"Truth" in Latin*

Vicky *Short for Victoria*

Victoria *Victory, feminine for Victor*

Viola *A violet, nickname Vi*

Violet *A plant with bright flowers, also Viola or Vi*

Virginia *Southern state in the United States, also Ginny*

Vivian *The enchantress and mistress of Merlin the magician in the King Arthur legends, French for "lively"*

Vogue *Stylish, fashionable*

Waif *Stray, homeless, name for a cat adopted from an animal shelter, variation Wafer, as in "cookie"*

Wampum *String of beads made of shells used by Native Americans for ornaments and money*

Wanda *The wanderer*

Wendy *A variation of Wanda*

Whimsy *Fanciful humor*

Whitney *Singer Whitney Houston, mountain in California*

Whoopee *A shout of glee, happiness*
Wiggles *A very active, wiggly cat*
Wilma *English name, short for Wilhelmina, Fred Flintstone's wife in the animated cartoon series* The Flintstones
Winfrey *Oprah Winfrey*
Winnie *Winnie the Pooh, bear in story by A. A. Milne*
Winona *Sioux for firstborn daughter*
Wintery *A good name for a white cat*
Wooly *For the cat with messy hair*
Wriggler *For the cat who moves around a lot*
Wunderkind *A good name for a very intelligent cat*

Xandra *Variation of Alexandra*
Xaveria *Unique, exotic feminine name*
Xenia *Greek meaning "hospitable to strangers," also Xena, Zena*
Xmas *For a cat received as a Christmas present*

Yakira *Hebrew for "expensive"*
Yara *Brazilian name thought to be derived from "January"*
Yin *The feminine principle in Chinese cosmology*
Ylang-Ylang *A tree with very fragrant greenish-yellow flowers*
Ynez *Spanish feminine name*

Yoko *Yoko Ono, wife of John Lennon*
Youngling *For a cat with a playful, youthful personality*
Yum-Yum *A good name for a cat that likes to eat*
Yva *A fantasy name*
Yvette *French name, original meaning "oak tree, acorn"*

Zara *Prosperous, also Zarah*
Zarpa *Spanish for "claw" or "paw"*
Zenobia *Ancient queen of Palmyra*
Zenzi *Short for Innozentia*
Zinfandel *A red wine from California*
Zerlinda *Calm, beautiful*
Zesty *For a cat that's full of life*
Zeta *Actress Katherine Zeta-Jones, also the sixth letter of the Greek alphabet*
Zigzag *Design, path, also Ziggy*
Zoey *Meaning "life"*
Zsa Zsa *Movie star Zsa Zsa Gabor*

JADE THE CHATTERBOX

Jade has mastered the "Meow" in many variations, all the way from the demanding "Meeeeow" to the long, drawn-out "Maaaa," which means roughly, "Please pay attention to me." As a greeting, I usually hear only a short "Meh." But woe is me if I'm slow to grasp that she wants to go out. Then a piercing "Ow" (the "Me" is dropped) ensues. Jade adores telling stories, and I listen . . .

INDEX

A Astrology   15

B Black cats, names for
22
Breed association for cats
14
Breeding Cats   14
Breeding Certificate   14

C Cat and human   12
Cat breeding   14
Cat horoscope   15
Cat stories   21, 23, 26, 28,
30, 35, 37, 38, 42, 45
Cats and children   7
Cats in film and on TV
10
Cats in literature   10
Cattery names   14
Celebrities and their cats
11
Changing the name   7
Choosing a name   5
Comic-strip cats   10

E Eternal child   9
Embarrassing names   6

F Famous cats   10
Females, names for
33–45

H Horoscope for cats   15

L Learning its name   5, 16,
17
Learning to understand
12
Long-haired cats, names
for   43
Lovable adventurers   9

M Male, names for   20–32
Misunderstandings   13

N Names for adventurers
32
Names for black cats   22
Names for females
33–45
Names for long-haired
cats   43
Names for males   20–32
Names for princes and
princesses   27
Names for red cats   44
Names for sensitive little
creatures   36
Names for smarties and
softies   29
Names for sociable
females   40
Names for the eternal
child   34
Names for twosomes   24
Names for white cats   33
Names for zodiac signs
25, 31, 39, 41
Names from A to Z
20–45
Nicknames   6

O Observing   12

P Pedigree   14
Pedigreed cats   14
Personality types   8, 9
Prince and princess   8

Q Quotes about cats   11

R Red cats, names for   44
Responsiveness   13
Rewards   17

S Scolding   17
Sensitive little creatures
8
Show catalog   14
Smarty and softie   8
Sociable feline   9

T Taboo names   7
Teaching the name   16,
17
Ten very common names
20
Tone of voice   12, 16, 17
Training   12
Twosomes, names for   24

U Unmistakable names
10, 17

W White cats, names for
33
Writers and cats   10, 11

Z Zodiac signs   15

ADDRESSES

General Organizations

North American Cat Registries

➤ American Association of Cat Enthusiasts (AACE)
P. O. Box 213
Pine Brook, NJ 07058
(973) 335-6717
www.aaceinc.org

➤ American Cat Association (ACA)
8101 Katherine Avenue
Panorama City, CA 91402
(818) 781-5656

➤ American Cat Fanciers Association (ACFA)
P. O. Box 203
Point Lookout, MO 65276
(417) 334-5430
www.acfacat.com

➤ Canadian Cat Association (CCA)
220 Advance Boulevard, Suite 101
Brampton, Ontario L6T 4J5
Canada
(905) 459-1481
www.cca-afc.com

➤ Cat Fanciers' Association (CFA)
1805 Atlantic Avenue
P. O. Box 1005
Manasquan, NJ 08736
(732) 528-9797
www.cfainc.org

➤ Cat Fanciers' Federation (CFF)
Box 661
Gratis, OH 45330
(937) 787-9009
www.cffinc.org

➤ National Cat Fanciers' Association (NCFA)
10215 West Mount Morris Road
Flushing, MI 48433
(810) 659-9517

➤ The International Cat Association (TICA)
P. O. Box 2684
Harlingen, TX 78551
(956) 428-8046
www.tica.org

➤ United Feline Organization (UFO)
P. O. Box 3234
Lacey, WA 98509-3234
(360) 438-6903

Miscellaneous Organizations

➤ American Humane Society
P. O. Box 1266
Denver, CO 80201
(303) 695-0811

➤ American Society for the Prevention of Cruelty to Animals (ASPCA)
424 East 92nd Street
New York, NY 10128
(212) 876-7700

➤ Food and Drug Administration's Center for Veterinary Medicine (FDA-CVM)
7500 Standish Place
Rockville, MD 20855

Books

➤ Behrend, A. *Cats.* Hauppauge, New York: Barron's Educational Series, Inc., 1999.

➤ Davis, Karen Leigh. *Compatible Cats.* Hauppauge, New York: Barron's Educational Series, Inc., 2001.

➤ _____. *The Cat Handbook.* Hauppauge, New York: Barron's Educational Series, Inc., 2000.

➤ Eden, Alex. *Cats Do the Cutest Things.* Hauppauge, New York: Barron's Educational Series, Inc., 2004.

➤ Helgren, J. Anne. *Encyclopedia of Cat Breeds: A Complete Guide to the Domestic Cats of North America.* Hauppauge, New York: Barron's Educational Series, Inc., 1997.

Magazines

➤ *CATS Magazine*
Editorial Office
260 Madison Avenue
New York, NY 10016
(917) 256-2200
➤ *Cat Fancy*
Editorial Office
P. O. Box 6050
Mission Viejo, CA 92690
➤ *Cat Fancier's Almanac*
Cat Fanciers' Association
1805 Atlantic Avenue
P. O. Box 1005
Manasquan, NJ 08736
(732) 528-9797
➤ *CATsumer Report*
P. O. Box 10069
Austin, TX 78766
(800) 968-1738

THE AUTHORS

For many years Gabriele
Linke-Grün has worked as a
freelance journalist for various pet magazines and
schoolbook publishers. She
works for Gräfe und Unzer
Verlag as a freelance editor
and reader of manuscripts,
and now as an author as
well. She has a liking for
cats: she grew up with them
and has always been fascinated by their strong indi-
vidualism and elegance.

Sharon Vanderlip, D.V.M.,
has written books and published articles in scientific
and general interest publica-
tions. Dr. Vanderlip served
as the Associate Director of
Veterinary Services for the
University of California at
San Diego School of
Medicine, and is the recipi-
ent of various awards for
her writing and dedication
to animal health.

THE PHOTOGRAPHERS

Artemis View/Elsner: page
8c, back cover l;
Giel: page 18;
Juniors/Schanz: page 8l;
Kuhn: page 30;
Prawitz: page 9r;
Schanz: pages 3tr, 11, 16, 17,
32, 37, 42;
Wegler: front cover, inside
front cover, pages 2, 3tl, b, 4,
7, 8r, 9l, c, 13, 14, 21, 23, 25,
26, 29, 35, 38, 41, 45, back
cover t, r.

First edition for the United
States, its territories and
dependencies, and Canada
published in 2005 by Barron's
Educational Series, Inc.

Copyright © 2003 by Gräfe und
Unzer Verlag, GmbH, Munich.
Originally published in
German under the title *1000
Katzennamen von A biz Z.*

English-language translation
copyright © 2005 by Barron's
Educational Series, Inc.

Translated from the German by
Kathleen Luft.

*All inquiries should be
addressed to:*
Barron's Educational Series, Inc.
250 Wireless Boulevard
Hauppauge, NY 11788
www.barronseduc.com

International Standard Book
No. 0-7641-3070-6

Library of Congress Catalog
Card No. 2004110793

Printed in China
9 8 7 6 5 4 3 2 1

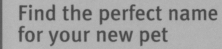

Find the perfect name for your new pet

➤ 1000 imaginative suggestions to get you started

➤ Find names that match your cat's appearance and personality

➤ Encourage the whole family to take part in pet naming

➤ Give your cat a name that says something about your own interests

➤ Pick out several favorites, then try them on your new pet

➤ See how your cat responds to each name

➤ It's a fun way to find your new pet's name

ISBN 0-7641-3070-6

UPC

0 27011 03070 3

www.barronseduc.com